LADIES'

Christian Commissions:

AUXILIARY TO THE

U. S. CHRISTIAN COMMISSION.

PHILADELPHIA:
C. SHERMAN, SON & CO., PRINTERS.
1864.

THIS record of the first step in the national movement for the organization of Ladies' Christian Commissions is sent forth as an embodiment of the plan and purpose for which it was set on foot.

The United States Christian Commission in sending it forth desires to express the satisfaction it has given and the hope it has inspired.

The general favor expressed, and the generous interest manifested by both ministers and people, and especially by the ladies, give promise of abundant success, which will insure a large revenue for the work of relief and benefit to our heroic soldiers.

To the memorial of the ladies the Commission would add an earnest request to the minister and the ladies of each congregation to organize and report without delay.

☞ *A request addressed to the United States Christian Commission Central Office,* 11 *Bank Street, Philadelphia, or any of the Branch Offices named on page* 24, *will secure copies of this Circular, the "Ladies' Christian Commissions," for local distribution.*

A NATIONAL MOVEMENT

FOR ORGANIZING

LADIES' CHRISTIAN COMMISSIONS.

On Wednesday morning, May 4th, a meeting of Ladies of the various Evangelical Denominations of the city, was held at Concert Hall, Philadelphia, for the purpose of adopting measures for the organization of Ladies' Christian Commissions in the various Churches throughout the country.

The Rev. Bishop Simpson, of the Methodist Episcopal Church, Philadelphia, was called to the chair, and Rev. Edward Lounsberry, of the Episcopal Church, appointed Secretary. Rev. J. Addison Henry, of the Presbyterian Church, led in prayer; after which Rt. Rev. Charles P. McIlvaine, D.D., Bishop of Ohio, and Rev. Robert J. Parvin, of Philadelphia, addressed the meeting. These gentlemen were followed by the Rev. Dr. Kirk, of the Congregational Church, Boston, who delivered the following address:

ADDRESS OF REV. DR. KIRK.

Sisters in Christ: Permit me, before introducing the subject specifically under the consideration of this meeting, to make a general suggestion in regard to the times in which we are living. The child of God should be more patriotic and loyal than others, should feel the nation's woes and perils with peculiar sensitiveness. Yes, the Christian, of all men, should feel his little bark tossing on the tempestuous sea which threatens the destruction of his country. But that feeling of solicitude and sorrow should in him be tempered and modified by another. He can neither sorrow nor fear as those who have no hope in God. He has confidence that God's providence is moving the world forward, and not backward. He has no fears for himself; for he will outlive society and its institutions; and his home is in "the city that hath foundations, whose builder and maker is God."

There was a woman, who, whatever she was or was not, whatever she did or failed to do, had made up her mind to love Jesus her Redeemer with her whole heart. Nothing was too precious to give him; no expression of love or gratitude to him could be extravagant. But what could she do? There were no rules laid down by the Church to guide her. There were no recognized models for her to imitate. What then did she do? She consulted her own heart, and that told her what to do. But there was, after all, no great value in the act she did perform. The Lord, indeed, made a kindly interpretation of it, when he said that she had done this for the day of his burial. But it had no real value in that direction, for God was not to suffer his Holy One to see corruption. Let us then look at the act, and his sentence pronounced upon it when it was censured. This woman purchased an alabaster-box of costly perfume, and carried it to the house where Jesus was entertained at a supper. Breaking the box, she poured the precious contents on his sacred person, washing his feet with her grateful tears, and wiping them with her hair.

When Jesus heard the cold, cynical, selfish grumbler object to the action, what was his reply? A precious sentence:

"She hath done what she could." That is enough, humble, obscure, diffident sister. To meet his approval, you are not to seek nor gain that of any other; you are not to imitate or equal any other; you are not necessarily even to escape the censure of others. Do what you can for Christ.

But who is to measure your ability? One who, for your sake, exchanged a throne for a gibbet; who, to secure your life, gave himself to death; one who thoroughly reads the heart; one who requires no brilliant display of affection, but rightly interprets a tear or a sigh; who puts a high value upon a little box of ointment, an unobserved desire to touch only the hem of his robe, a cup of cold water given in his name, or two mites thrown into his treasury.

BUT, WHAT CAN YOU DO?

What can the weakest or obscurest do? First of all, you can love your Redeemer, and consecrate yourself to his service. He is worthy of all, and infinitely more than you can render. Give it to him, all the wealth and strength of your love and confidence. Give him the first place, and then every human being can have his proper place. Live in him; live for him.

Love to our Lord and Saviour should always, but especially in this day of rebuke and chastisement, take on the form of humility. The divine injunction is: "Humble yourselves under the mighty hand of God." It is a hand so broad you cannot escape from its grasp; so "mighty," you cannot successfully resist its pressure. Struggling and fretting but increase the pain. Submit; that is our duty and our policy. Go down. How low? Until you reach the other hand; for "underneath are the everlasting arms." And the aim of Infinite Goodness is simply this: to continue the pressure until there is nothing but God to lean upon. We must go down through creatures and idols and our own strength, until we touch the supporting hand,—then the crushing hand will cease its pressure. This is the method of Infinite Love, when it has purposed our highest good. But, will he not sink me, or the beloved institutions of my country, and with them the hope of the world, into the abyss? No; he is jealous of your confidence, and desires to be its supreme object. Humble yourselves in this day of your country's calamity. If the Ninevites could consent to fast, and clothe themselves in sackcloth at the call of a strange prophet, surely the Christian women of the Republic can consent to express a sympathy with their suffering and imperilled country, by self-denial in dress and food; by simplicity in both, to give outward and appropriate expression to their grief for sins which have so provoked their beloved Redeemer, and called forth from him such expressions of displeasure.

To put it on the lowest ground, it is in bad taste to increase the splendor of dress and furniture, and the luxury of living, when our country, as dear to us as our kindred, lies sick unto death.

And this leads me to show another good thing each of you can do. Love your country, and judge the character of others in part, by their regard for it. Love your country, and willingly sacrifice anything its interests demand. If economy in dress and living will affect the value of our currency, and tend to save the financial credit of the Government, let there be no hesitation. If Southern women will dress in calicoes for such a government as their leaders are seeking to establish, surely Northern women can do as much for our Government. Love your country. It is worthy of your love. None ever was more so. Its institutions, its national character, its relations to the human race, and its coming history, its relations to the church of Christ, all claim for it a high place in our affections. Bear its sorrows on your heart. Regard it as you do a sick child, with a never interrupted sympathy; carrying its pain into your very sleep with you.

Identify yourself with the soldier who is defending that country. It matters not who the man is that occupies that sacred post; for the time being, and as such, place him in your inner heart. Count his family yours, so as to share with them their sorrows and solicitudes.

You can not over-estimate the power of your sex in certain directions. It seems to me that one of the strongest forces in this rebellion is, the devotion of the women of the Southern States to what they call their country and its cause. Blind, misguided and wicked as it is, yet, like the Satan of Milton, it is admirable in its energy and self-sacrificing persistency. It has been said that the shrewd plotters of this villany if rightly estimating this power, took care in their chosen mates to fire the hearts of the Southern women; that Mr. Brooks was by them goaded on to make his brutal attack on Mr. Sumner. And we saw in the early history of the war, how powerful was the stimulus of their zeal on the hearts of sons and brothers, husbands and friends. We hear of the richest of them at this day suppressing the desire of dressing according to their taste and ability, that they may have the means of ministering to their starving soldiers. In itself this is noble. And shall not the women of the North at least equal them, if not surpass them in this?

Might not every lady send a letter to the army every month; not only to kindred there, but to friends, or even strangers? The times and circumstances would remove from it every shade of impropriety. Ascertain if any young man from your neighborhood is without friends, or if a family find it difficult to write frequently to the husband and father. Be in such cases the amanuensis for all your loyal sisters, and frequently write a letter to such. Tell them about home; tell them about their neighbors. Be cheerful, even entertaining in your communications. Put not a line of disaster or fear in them. Be kind, and above all, let them see that you are chiefly anxious for their eternal welfare. You may have heard much said about the value of letters to a soldier; but you cannot overestimate it.

Pray for your country, the government, the army, and the navy.

Sisters, do you know how wonderful, how glorious a reality is prayer! Have you searched the Scriptures to see what a channel of the divine power God has been pleased to make it?

But what is prayer? It is the heart, not the head, uttering itself to God. It is the soul pleading in the name of Christ, for great blessings which God alone can bestow. Wherein lies its power? In these elements, desire, humility, confidence, thankfulness. Specific and strong desiring is the essence of prayer; always consenting to be refused, always preferring God's will to its own; yet specific and earnest in desiring. This comparison was once made in my hearing. A mother, passing a room where her children were playing, heard one of them crying. But the quick instinct of a mother's heart told her the child was not grieved. It was play-cry. Repassing the room she heard another cry. This turned her step quick as thought to the sufferer. That was a real cry; a heart-tone was in it. Too often we have play-cry. When our hearts are burdened and grieved, there is a Father's ear quick to hear it.

Mark that child climbing up to its father's lap, throwing its little arms around his neck. Tell me if that is not a position of power. He may be a man whose will sways the mind of a nation, on whose eloquence that nation waits for impulse and guidance. But, in the strong language of Scripture, that child takes hold upon the strength of that strong man. Such is prayer. Except ye be converted and become as little children, ye have no power in prayer.

Pray, sisters; pray for your country, for the men who guide it, and the men who defend it. Be simple, be earnest, be humble, be bold with a holy "boldness to enter into the holiest by the blood of Jesus?" "With thanksgiving let your request be made known in the name of Jesus."

All this you certainly can do, whatever station you occupy, however limited the gift intrusted to you by the Lord, who accepts "according to what a man hath."

Now, let me suggest to you one other course of action. Do what you can to sustain the Christian Commission. You know its work and its claims. None of all the funds of Christian beneficence is, for the time, paramount to it.

And we now propose to you a course which, while severely taxing no individual, will secure immense results. Within your own parish see to it that a society be organized, if agreeable to the officers and members of the Church, to secure a yearly subscription in money, and such labor for the army as the Central Committee, from time to time, may show to be needed for furnishing the soldiers with hospital garments. See to it that while the necessity for this kind of effort shall continue, your association be kept in vigorous operation.

And when your account is made by Him whose favor is life, may it be

"She hath done what she could."

Remarks were also made by Rev. J. E. Cheshire, of the Baptist Church, Rev. A. G. McAuley, of the Reformed Presbyterian Church, Rev. Dr. Newton, and Rev. R. G. Matlack, of the Episcopal Church.

Rev. J. G. Maxwell read the following resolutions, which were unanimously adopted:

Resolved, As the unanimous expression of the sentiment of this meeting that we recommend to ladies of the various Evangelical Churches in the loyal States, that they organize Ladies' Christian Commissions in each congregation, auxiliary to the United States Christian Commission.

Resolved, That the United States Christian Commission be requested to issue a circular embodying a form of organization, with hints as to the process of organizing.

Resolved, That we recommend that the terms of membership for these auxiliaries be fixed at $1 per annum.

MEMORIAL

To Christian Ladies and Christian Ministers.

The Loyal Christian Women of our beloved country have done, and are doing a great deal to relieve, cheer, and save the noble men who are exposing their own lives to save the life of the Nation, and they are ready to do still more as opportunity may offer. Of them, and for them, we may confidently say, that nothing will be left undone, which Christian women can with propriety possibly do, to promote either the bodily welfare or religious benefit of those who fight the battles of our nation.

The loyal Christian women of our beloved country will take double pleasure in honoring our dear Redeemer while they bless the defenders of the Union, and relieve those who suffer in its cause. It will give them the profoundest joy to add to the cup of cold water ministered to the thirsty soldier on the field of blood, the Christian grace of having it given by a disciple of Jesus, and accompanied by the comforting words of salvation. If, while they aid in saving the nation by saving, cheering, strengthening its defenders, and serve the cause of humanity by mitigating anguish and ministering comfort to the sick, the wounded, the dying, they can at the same time in all they do, glorify the precious Saviour who died for us, their delight will be full, their reward abundant.

Happily, a plan has been formed, which, if carried out, cannot fail of honoring the Saviour, benefiting the soldier, and nelping the country on a truly national scale. The United States Christian Commission needs the organized aid of the ladies to supply money and stores for its work, and a national movement has commenced with a view to the organization of a Ladies' Christian Commission in each evangelical congregation of the whole country not in rebellion, with an annual membership fee of one dollar for each member.

The excellence of this plan will be seen at a glance.

1. First, in its perfect feasibility. Few churches will refuse to enter into it. Most of them will rejoice in placing themselves side by side with the great body of the churches of our Lord Jesus in so great a movement and so good a work. Few, if any, who love our Saviour, our country, and the brave men of our army and navy, will refuse to aid by giving their names and the small fee required.

2. Second, in its remarkable economy. Most churches will probably act in the matter at once, and proceed to organize spontaneously. And, if necessary, there are amongst the ladies enough who will cheerfully visit, without salary, such churches as need any one to aid them in organizing, and thus this grëat national movement can be thoroughly carried out without the expense of a salaried agency.

3. Third, in its grand results. If generally adopted, it will

enlist the organized aid of nearly all in all our evangelical congregations, present the whole church united in one grand work of patriotic Christian benevolence, and secure to the United States Christian Commission an immense fund, not less than a million of dollars, for the unlimited expansion and vigorous prosecution of its great work in all parts of the army and navy.

As a Committee, appointed by the ladies of Philadelphia, and charged with the duty of memorializing the ladies of all the loyal States, we lay this matter before you, and solicit your hearty co-operation in the movement. Accompanying this memorial you will find the form of a constitution, purposely made short, comprehensive, and plain, which, if need be, you can change in any particular to suit the circumstances of your own church. Pastor and ladies uniting, a Commission can be formed without delay in each church, and a little pains on the part of both, and especially on the part of the ladies, will serve to secure all members of the congregation as members of the Commission.

This done, the first great object of the movement will have been accomplished. A grand Christian national organization will have been secured, and means will have been easily, largely, and economically accumulated. And this can be done without subverting, changing, or limiting any other organization which may have been already formed before.

Beyond this, the Commission when organized in any congregation not already engaged in the work through some other channel, can adopt measures for gathering and preparing stores, and thus render material aid to the United States Christian Commission by the contribution of stores to be distributed by its delegates, or to supply its diet kitchens in connection with the great hospitals in the field.

May we not confidently rely upon prompt and efficient action on the part of all Christian ladies and Christian ministers in aid, by all suitable means, of this national Christian movement?

Baptist.

CHURCH.	LADY REPRESENTING SAME.
First, ...	Mrs. A. S. Larcumb.
Fourth, ...	Mrs. Rev. J. R. Jeffery.
Fifth, ...	Mrs. Howard Malcomb.
Tenth, ...	Miss B. L. Kennard.
Eleventh, ...	Mrs. J. Hyatt Smith.
Berean, ...	Mrs. Rev. J. Cooper.
Blockley, ...	Mrs. Rev. W. H. H. Marsh.
Broad Street, ...	Mrs. Rev. P. S. Henson.
Lower Dublin, . . .	Mrs. Dr. Anderson.
Roxborough, ...	Mrs. H. C. Jones.
Schuylkill Falls, . . .	Mrs. J. E. Cheshire.
Spring Garden, . . .	Mrs. Tusland.
Spruce Street, . . .	Miss F. Annable.
West Philadelphia, . .	Mrs. Rev. J. H. Castle.

New School Presbyterian.

CHURCH.	LADY REPRESENTING SAME.
First, Washington Square, .	Mrs. W. H. Hilderburn.
First, Southwark, . . .	Mrs. J. M. Dorman.
First, Northern Liberties, .	Mrs. Heilman.
First, Kensington, . . .	Mrs. Rev. William T. Eva.
First, West Philadelphia, .	Mrs. E. C. Warren.
First, Mantua, . . .	Mrs. H. W. Baltz.
Third, ...	Mrs. James Frasier.
Twelfth, ...	Mrs. Rev. R. A. Malery.
Calvary, ...	Mrs. Rev. Dr. Malan.
Central Northern Liberties, .	Mrs. Rev. J. G. Mitchell.
Clinton Street, . . .	Mrs. Rev. D. March.
Logan Square, . . .	Mrs. J. Patton.
Market Square, . . .	Mrs. O. Dean.
North Broad, ...	Mrs. Thomas Potter.
Olivet, ...	Mrs. W. W. Taylor.
Southwestern, . . .	Mrs. John Cowan.
Tabor Prebyterian, . .	Mrs. G. Van Deurs.
Western, ...	Mrs. William E. Tenbrook.

Moravian.

CHURCH.	LADY REPRESENTING SAME.
Moravian, ...	Mrs. Rev. A. A. Reincke.

Dutch Reformed.

First, ...	Mrs. Rev. J. H. Suydam.
Second, ...	Mrs. Rev. T. De Witt Talmage.
Third, ...	Mrs. Daniel S. Jones.
Fourth, ...	Mrs. Rev. William Fulton.

Methodist Episcopal.

MRS. BISHOP SIMPSON.

Arch Street, ...	Mrs. George Cookman.
Asbury, ...	Mrs. E. Cooper.
Broad Street,. . . .	Mrs. Butler.
Central, ...	Mrs. R. Ervine.
Ebenezer, ...	Mrs. Early.
Eleventh Street, . . .	Mrs. A. Cather.
Fifth Street, ...	Mrs. Scott.
Green Street,. . . .	Mrs. J. H. McFarland.
Hedding, ...	Mrs. Rev. A. Manship.
Salem, ...	Mrs. Henry.
Sanctuary, ...	Mrs. Maclay.
Spring Garden, . . .	Mrs. A. W. Rand.
St. John's, ...	Mrs. Long.
Tabernacle, ...	Mrs. P. Coombe.
Trinity, ...	Mrs. Alexander Cummings.
Union, ...	Mrs. Hammett.
Western, ...	Mrs. Jones.
Wharton Street, . . .	Mrs. Rev. J. F. Chaplain.

Reformed Presbyterian.

Broad Street,. . . .	Mrs. R. S. J. Black.
Cherry Street, . . .	Mrs. Stephenson.
Deal Street, ...	Mrs. W. Young.
Hancock Street, . . .	Mrs. Patton.
York Street, ...	Mrs. Rev. A. G. McAuley.
Seventeenth Street, . .	Mrs. Rev. S. O. Wylie.
Eighteenth Street,. . .	Mrs. Rev. D. Steel.
Twenty-second Street, . .	Mrs. Rev. William Sterrett.

German Reformed.

CHURCH.	LADY REPRESENTING SAME.
First, ...	Mrs. Dr. J. H. Bomberger.
Bethlehem, ...	Mrs. Rev. J. G. Newber.
Christ Church, ...	Mrs. S. H. Giesy.
St. Stephen's, ...	Mrs. Rev. A. Ronick.
Zion, ...	Mrs. Rev. N. Gehr.
West Philadelphia, . .	Mrs. Rev. J. Dahlman.

United Presbyterian.

First, ...	Miss C. Church.
Second, ...	Mrs. Rev. Dr. Dales.
Third, ...	Mrs. Rev. Dr. Cooper.
Fifth, ...	Mrs. Rev. T. H. Hanna.
Sixth, ...	Miss Young.
Seventh, ...	Miss E. D. J. Hoagland.
Shippen Street, ...	Mrs. Lunney.
Mission, ...	Miss McNeil.

Protestant Episcopal.

All Saints, ...	Mrs. Mary Soby.
Calvary, ...	Mrs. Robbins.
Church of the Advent, . .	Mrs. Abel Reed & Miss Jane Baker.
Church of the Atonement, .	Mrs. Ashton.
Church of the Epiphany, .	Mrs. Rev. Dr. Newton.
Church of the Holy Trinity, .	Mrs. William Bucknell.
Church of the Intercessor, .	Mrs. R. O. Lowry.
Church of the Mediator, .	Mrs. F. Hoskins.
Church of the Nativity, . .	Mrs. Rev. C. Matlack.
Emanuel, ...	Mrs. Leib.
Grace, ...	Mrs. Yarrow.
St. Andrew's,.	Mrs. M. G. Smith.
St. Jude's, ...	Miss Anna E. Conarroe.
St. Peter's, ...	Miss Mary Clarkson.
St. Mark's, Frankford, . .	Mrs. D. S. Miller.
St. Mary's, ...	Miss J. A. Wiltberger.
St. Philip's, ...	Mrs. Rev. C. D. Cooper.
St. Paul's, ...	Mrs. Jay Cooke.
St. Luke's, Thirteenth Street,	Mrs. George Harris.

Congregational.

CHURCH.	LADY REPRESENTING SAME.
First, ...	Mrs. Burdett Heart.
Independent, ...	Mrs. J. C. Hunter.

Lutheran.

St. Matthew's, . . .	Mrs. Rev. Dr. Hutter.
St. Michael's, . . .	Mrs. E. F. A. Schaeffer.

Old School Presbyterian.

Second, ...	Mrs. Daniel Haddock.
Second, Germantown, . .	Mrs. J. G. Mitchell.
Fourth, ...	Mrs. William Rice.
Seventh, ...	Mrs. Clifford Smith, Jr.
Ninth, ...	Mrs. William Patterson.
Tenth, ...	Mrs. Mary Milligan.
Fifteenth, ...	Mrs. William McElwee.
Alexander, ...	Mrs. Rev. T. M. Cunningham.
Arch Street, ...	Miss O'Neil.
Cohocksink, ...	Mrs. E. Hatch.
Frankford, ...	Mrs. Rev. T. Murphy.
Holmesburg, ...	Mrs. Jacob Bellville.
North, ...	Mrs. E. A. Halloway.
Penn, ...	Mrs. Jefferson Lewis.
Princeton, ...	Mrs. W. T. Snodgrass.
Scots', ...	Mrs. Cunningham.
South, ...	Mrs. H. A. Moore.
Spring Garden, . . .	Mrs. Morris C. Sutphen.
Union, ...	Mrs. Rev. Robert Gamble.
West Arch Street, . . .	Mrs. Rev. J. Edwards.
West Spruce Street, . .	Mrs. C. H. Grant.
First German, . . .	Mrs. Arch. McIntyre.

Committee of Arrangements.

Miss Rachel Wetherell, *Chairman.*
Mrs. Kelley, *Secretary.*
Mrs. Rev. J. H. Suydam.
Miss O. Neil.
Mrs. Alex. Cummings.
Mrs. Rev. Dr. Dale.
Miss F. Annable.
Mrs. J. H. Jackson.
Mrs. Rev. Dr. Bomberger.
Miss St. Clair.

FORM OF CONSTITUTION

FOR

LADIES' CHRISTIAN COMMISSIONS.

Ladies' Christian Commission of
Auxiliary to the United States Christian Commission for the Army and Navy.

ARTICLE I. The officers of this Commission shall be a President, Vice-President, Secretary, and Treasurer, chosen annually from the ladies of the congregation, but to hold office until others shall be elected.

ARTICLE II. Any member of the congregation, man, woman, or child, may become a member of this Commission by the payment of *One Dollar* annually into its treasury.

ARTICLE III. All money received for membership fees shall be paid over to the (*) United States Christian Commission, for its general work, and go into a national "Membership Fund."

ARTICLE IV. All moneys received by this Commission in contributions over and above membership fees, and from every other source, shall, after making therefrom all necessary purchases, and defraying needful expenses, be paid over to the United States Christian Commission for the general work, and go toward another national fund, to be known as the "Donation Fund."

ARTICLE V. An annual meeting shall be held on the
of , of which notice shall be given at some previous pub-

* If report is made to any Branch of the U. S. Christian Commission, here give its name.

lic meeting of the congregation. Full reports of the affairs of this Commission shall be made by the Secretary and Treasurer, and an election of officers shall be held at each annual meeting.

ARTICLE VI. This constitution may be altered or amended at any annual meeting, provided public notice is given at the time the notice of the meeting is given, that such alteration or amendment will be proposed.

SUGGESTIONS.

To carry out the National plan of Ladies' Christian Commissions fully, it will be necessary, 1. To form a Commission in each separate congregation. 2. To have each Commission directly auxiliary to the United States Christian Commission, or some one of its branches. 3. To have the organization reported in full to the United States Christian Commission, or the Branch with which the Ladies' Commission connects itself, together with the name of the *Ladies' Commission* and the *names of its officers.* 4. To have the amount paid in for admission fees paid over directly to the United States Christian Commission, or the Branch to which the Ladies' Commission attaches itself as auxiliary. If money is needed for the purchase of materials to make up, or for carrying on the work in the locality where the Ladies' Commission is situated, let it be secured in some other way, so as to leave the general *membership fund* unreduced. The Ladies' Christian Commissions should not only swell this fund as largely as possible, but have full credit for it in the reports of the United States Christian Commission, and in the history of the day.

In carrying out this plan it is not at all necessary that those who become members of a Ladies' Christian Commission should cease to be members of any other association in the same church or community, designed to benefit the soldier either through the United States Christian Commission, or any other agency in the field. It is not necessary that a Ladies' Christian Commission should in every case be a society for gathering stores, or making up garments, however desirable that might be in itself. Two great objects will be attained by getting all to become members,—the *membership fund* will be augmented by the fees paid in, and all will be combined in the great National Christian Commission. If to these the further benefit can be added of having stores gathered and garments prepared, that will be well; but although important it is not indispensable. Let every church organize, and every member of the congregation join. And then, whatever else can be done will be so much gained.

Much, however, may be done by the ladies in addition to the means they gather by membership fees and the interest they enlist, by combining great numbers in the Commission. They may encourage their ministers in the successful establishment of monthly soldiers' meetings with monthly collections, as proposed by the United States Christian Commission. They may meet and make up clothing, &c., for the soldiers. They may gather in stores, and they may solicit and secure contributions in addition to the fees of those who become members. They may secure for the great work of the United States Christian Commission besides the "Membership Fund," another, possibly as large, to be known as the "Donation Fund," both of which, in the reports and history of the benevolence called forth by the sad exigencies of this terrible war, will be known distinctively as part of what has been done by woman.

SECOND PHILADELPHIA MEETING.

A Large and Enthusiastic Gathering.

THE plan of establishing Ladies' Christian Commissions throughout the loyal churches of the land, under the encouragement and co-operation of the Christian Commission, has met with great favor. The movement has begun in nearly all the larger cities, and is expected to embrace every community. Two great objects are to be secured by this movement: first, the union of the Christians of the North, and West, and East, as members of the Christian Commission; secondly, largely increased means for the prosecution of the Commission's work by membership fees, and by contributions secured by the ladies.

The meeting was held at Concert Hall, Philadelphia, on the morning of May 31. Short addresses were made by delegates who had just returned from the scenes of their holy mission, and reports were presented from the Ladies' Committees already at work.

Although the express purpose of this meeting was to complete the arrangements for sending out this memorial, yet so promptly and earnestly have the churches entered into the work, that the following contributions were unexpectedly handed in; the largest being only in part, and many of them but the small beginnings in the several congregations.

	Membership Fund.	Contribution Fund.	Total.
First Presbyterian Church, Kensington,	$500	$1 00	$501 00
Seventh Presbyterian Church,	248	20 00	268 00
Church of the Mediator,	195	105 00	300 00
Cohocksink Presbyterian Church,	14	50 00	64 00
Tenth Presbyterian Church,	196	87 15	283 15
West Spruce Street Presbyterian Church,	82	60 00	142 00
First Presbyterian Church, Dr. Barnes,	108	55 00	163 00
Princeton Presbyterian Church,	91	75 00	166 00
First Reformed Presbyterian Church,	60	8 50	68 50
First Baptist Church,	71		71 00
Second United Presbyterian Church,	97	31 00	128 00
First Reformed Dutch Church,	82		82 00
Union Presbyterian Church,	64	28 60	92 60
Calvary Monumental Church,	26		26 00
Third United Presbyterian Church,	44		44 00
Ladies' Christian Com., Holmesburg (add'l),	20	5 00	25 00
North Broad Street Presbyterian Church,	115	255 50	370 50
Church of the Epiphany (add'l),	20		20 00
Ninth Presbyterian Church,	175		175 00
Clinton Street Presbyterian Church,	140	10 00	150 00
Church of the Intercessor,	55	45 00	100 00
Ninth United Presbyterian Church,	35		35 00
	$2,448	$826 75	$3,274 75

INCIDENTS.

Of the thousands of intensely interesting incidents which are constantly transpiring, space will only allow us to give the following:

Sergeant John Crosby, of the 57th Regiment Massachusetts Volunteers, wounded five times with one ball, being attended by Dr. McClellan, exclaimed: "Oh, sir! I have $2000 in gold at home, which I will give you if you will dress my wound till I get well." Being assured that delegates' services were gratis, he said: "How glad I am to hear you pray: come and pray with me again."

Another young man, by the name of Josiah B. Hall, of the same regiment, wounded in the bowels, which Dr. McClellan dressed, and then gave him a cup of cocoa, he said: "I will write to my father, if he is a man, to join the Christian Commission."

On the damp ground at Falmouth lay a poor sufferer, whose body gave him no rest. Said he to the Rev. A. S. Twombly: "Please talk to me about those things (meaning God and heaven) some more." "I continued," says Mr. Twombly, "the conversation I had begun, when turning about I found him indeed *tranquilly asleep.*"

A dying boy from Venango County, Pa., said to a delegate as he took his hand and placed it on his breast, "Stay with me, oh! stay with me and talk of Jesus until I die." He fell asleep in that same Jesus at sundown.

A young man, from Vermont, suffering excruciating pain from the loss of his leg, said to the same delegate: "My sufferings are beyond language to describe; but the sweetness of the precious Jesus you have brought me exceeds them." With these words he closed his eyes on his earthly trials, to look upon the face of his Saviour.

Rev. Mr. Bringhurst tells us with what force the home-link of the Commission came upon him, during a visit to the White

House. He had been asked, by a lady of our city, to search for her absent brother, of whom she had heard nothing since the commencement of the May campaign. Going to the tents of the Fifth Army Corps, he noticed a young man lying upon the ground: stooping to administer to him he found him dead, whilst fastened to his coat was the name of the lady's brother. He ascertained the circumstances of his death, and, cutting a lock of hair for his sister, transmitted the sad tidings to her.

Many eminent physicians are sent out by the Commission, who render very important service. Among these were Drs. Reed, Goodman, and Parker. The latter reports that with his own hands he made three thousand dressings for wounds at Fredericksburg. The gratitude of the relieved for such labor cannot be expressed; yet this is only an instance among hundreds of like exertions.

The following is an instance of the unbounded confidence the soldiers have in the delegates of the Commission:

After the 2d Connecticut Regiment was paid off, they put their several packages into a bag and sent it to the Commission tent, only requesting that they be sent to their homes. On overhauling it, it was found to contain about seventeen thousand dollars, which was expressed to their friends at home. Hundreds of watches and other valuables are given to the delegates for safe keeping.

A delegate says: "I was repeatedly solicited to write letters for the helpless at this hospital. After several days of such labor, a young man of more than ordinarily interesting appearance, beckoned me to his cot, and requested me to write a few lines for him. I cordially assented, and asked to whom? He covered his face with his hand, and amid his sobs, exclaimed, "Oh! sir, I cannot tell my mother that my leg is gone; but I wish you would, and comfort her."

Said a soldier to Chaplain Thomas at Bermuda Hundred: "What a blessed institution this Christian Commission is! Your delegates care for us in the hospital, follow us on the march, and in the hour of battle they hover around us like ministering angels."

LADIES' CHRISTIAN COMMISSIONS

May report* to the U. S. CHRISTIAN COMMISSION, Central Office, 11 Bank Street, Philadelphia, or either of the following Branches:

NEW YORK, ...	Office, 30 Bible House.
BOSTON, ...	" 4 Court Street.
PITTSBURG, ...	" 71 Wood Street.
CINCINNATI, ...	" 51 Vine Street.
INDIANAPOLIS, IND.	
CHICAGO, ...	" Methodist Church Block.
ST. LOUIS, ...	" under Lindell Hotel.
DETROIT.	
BALTIMORE, ...	" 77 West Baltimore Street.
BUFFALO, N. Y.	
PEORIA, ILL.	
PORTLAND, ME.	

* FORM OF REPORT.—Ladies' Christian Commission of the (give name and location of Church), auxiliary to the (give name of the Commission or Branch reported to). Officers: President, —— ——. Vice-President, —— ——. Secretary, —— ——. Treasurer, —— ——. Amount cash: Membership, $——. Donations, $——. Total, $——.

(Signed) —— ——,

Secretary.

www.ingramcontent.com/pod-product-compliance
Lightning Source LLC
LaVergne TN
LVHW011144110826
845150LV00008B/2499
* 9 7 8 1 4 1 8 1 9 2 4 9 5 *